A BUSINESS APPROACH TO PEA FARMING

Complete Entrepreneurial Step By Step Guide To Pea Garden From Scratch

ZHURI HART

DISCLAIMER

This book is intended to provide general information and insights on adopting a business approach to farming. The content within is based on the author's knowledge and experiences up to the date of publication. It is essential to recognize that the field of agriculture is dynamic, influenced by various factors such as market conditions, climate, and regulatory changes.

Readers are advised to conduct thorough research, seek professional advice, and consider their unique circumstances before implementing any strategies or practices discussed in this book. The author and publisher disclaim any responsibility for the accuracy, completeness, or suitability of the information provided. The book is not a substitute for professional advice, and the author and publisher shall not be liable for any damages or losses arising from the use or reliance on the information presented herein.

Individual results may vary, and success in farming enterprises is contingent upon numerous variables. The author encourages readers to consult with relevant experts, agricultural extension services, and legal or financial professionals to tailor strategies to their specific needs and local conditions.

This book is not intended to be a comprehensive guide to all aspects of farming, and readers should exercise their judgment and discretion in applying the principles discussed. The author and publisher do not endorse any specific products, services, or companies mentioned in this book unless explicitly stated.

By reading this book, the reader acknowledges and accepts the inherent uncertainties in agricultural endeavors and agrees to use the information at their own risk.

TABLE OF CONTENTS

ABOUT THE BOOK

"A Business Approach to Pea Farming" is a thorough manual that offers insightful analysis and useful tactics to anyone looking to enter the pea farming sector. The book starts with a thoughtful introduction that sets the scene for the significance of pea growing and defines its goals. It makes it obvious who its target market is, which includes both new and seasoned farmers as well as agricultural enthusiasts who want to learn more about the pea farming industry. The synopsis of the pea farming industry provides context for the detailed investigation that follows.

The basics of peas are covered in detail, along with their different varieties, nutritional value, market demand, and potential profitability. Making wise selections in the pea farming industry requires this fundamental information. After being discussed, market analysis takes on greater significance as it looks at customer preferences, industry trends, competitor analysis, and methods for locating niche markets.

This book gives readers the skills they need to successfully negotiate the competitive environment.

The book walks readers through the process of planning a pea farm, including site selection, soil preparation, and crop rotation techniques. This brings us to the practical side of pea farming. Important topics such as farm infrastructure and equipment, cultivation techniques, sustainable farming techniques, financial planning, marketing tactics, and legal issues are covered in the ensuing chapters. Every chapter offers a thorough examination of the subject matter while also providing expert guidance and useful suggestions that may be used right away in the field.

The growing significance of ecologically friendly methods in contemporary agriculture is reflected in the inclusion of a section devoted to sustainable farming practices. Furthermore, the book's overall usefulness is greatly enhanced by the chapters on financial planning and marketing tactics, which help users successfully manage their finances and promote their pea products.

In its concluding portion, the book also examines the future of pea growing, discussing new developments in technology, market trends, adaptation to climate change, and prospects and difficulties. This forward-looking viewpoint guarantees that readers will be ready to adjust to changing market trends.

"A Business Approach to Pea Farming" is a priceless tool for everybody involved in or curious about pea farming. It is a priceless resource for novices and seasoned professionals in the agriculture industry alike due to its organized methodology, comprehensive material, and useful suggestions.

CHAPTER ONE

PEA FARMING INTRODUCTION

RECOGNIZING PEAS

Peas are a versatile and nutrient-dense legume that has been a mainstay of meals for ages all across the world. Peas are complex plants, and learning about them requires investigating their different varieties, evaluating their nutritional worth, and determining the commercial need that motivates pea cultivation. Peas are a major actor in the agricultural landscape because of their potential profitability, which has attracted the attention of both farmers and agribusinesses.

Peas or Pisum sativum as they are officially defined, are legumes that are well known for their tiny, spherical seeds enclosed in pods. Usually holding many peas, these pods highlight the unique reproductive anatomy of the plant. Originating in the Neolithic period, peas have progressed from wild to cultivated forms and are now a staple food in many parts of the world. Understanding pea farming entails taking into account elements including growth patterns, climate, and soil requirements, underscoring the agronomic expertise necessary for productive cultivation.

PEA TYPES

The pea family is incredibly diverse, with many different varieties that suit diverse culinary tastes and farming methods. Sugar peas, commonly referred to as snap peas, snow peas, and garden peas, are included in the classification of peas. Because of their sweet flavor and edible pods, sugar peas are a popular addition to salads and stir-fries. In contrast, snow peas have delicate, flat pods and are frequently used in Asian cooking. When the peas inside the pod are fully developed, they are usually harvested. Garden peas are the familiar green peas that are found in many houses. Because each variety of pea has distinct qualities of its own, producers can choose varieties that meet customer preferences and market trends.

VALUE NUTRITIONALLY

Peas are prized for their remarkable nutritional profile in addition to their flavor. Peas are a great addition to a balanced and healthful diet since they are full of vital nutrients like vitamins, minerals, and fiber. They are an excellent source of protein, especially for vegetarians or those on plant-based diets. Furthermore, peas are a great source of vitamins A and C, which support healthy skin and a strong immune system. Dietary fiber, which is found in peas, facilitates digestion and supports gut health. Producers need to promote peas as a health-conscious food option as well as for consumers looking for a nutrient-dense diet to understand the nutritional worth of peas.

DEMAND FOR PEAS IN THE MARKET

Due to the growing awareness of health-conscious customer choices and the versatility of peas in a variety of culinary applications, the market demand for peas has grown steadily.

Peas are popular among consumers because of their varied culinary options, environmental sustainability as a crop that fixes nitrogen, and superior nutritional value. Fresh peas, canned peas, and frozen peas are in greater demand in domestic and international markets, giving producers the chance to satisfy rising consumer demands. Stakeholders hoping to profit from this demand must have a thorough understanding of the market dynamics, including consumer preferences, new trends, and the function of peas in the food processing industry.

PROSPECTIVE FINANCIAL SUCCESS

Pea growing has become a desirable alternative for farmers and agribusiness businesses due to its potential profitability. Due to its comparatively short growing season, peas can be harvested numerous times a year, increasing their economic viability. Their adaptability in terms of processing techniques and culinary applications also opens up opportunities for value addition, which raises profitability even further.

To optimize their profits, producers should investigate various market channels such as fresh product marketplaces, food processing enterprises, and export markets, given the increasing need for peas. Stakeholders hoping to succeed in the pea cultivation industry must comprehend the elements that affect profitability, such as effective farming techniques, pest control, and marketing tactics.

The complex network of knowledge about peas includes their variety, nutritional value, market demand, and prospective profitability. Given that peas are still regarded as a valuable crop in both traditional and modern agricultural settings, everyone involved in the production, marketing, or consumption of peas has to have a thorough understanding of these ideas.

CHAPTER TWO

EXAMINATION OF THE MARKET

SECTORAL PATTERNS

Comprehending industry trends is crucial for conducting an efficient market study. Industry trends are the current trends, advancements, and changes that are occurring in a particular industry. Technological developments, alterations in regulations, changes in the economy, and changes in society can all have an impact on these patterns. Businesses can anticipate market dynamics and modify their strategies accordingly by analyzing industry trends.

Companies should take into account noteworthy industry trends such as the shift towards artificial intelligence and the growing focus on sustainability in the technology sector. Keeping up with these developments guarantees that companies can take advantage of new chances and properly place themselves in the market.

CUSTOMER PREFERENCES

The tastes of consumers significantly influence the dynamics of the market. Businesses must comprehend the factors that influence consumer decisions, including product features, pricing, brand loyalty, and overall customer experience, to effectively customize their products. To find trends and preferences entails performing market research, surveying customers, and evaluating their responses. Consumer preferences are changing, as seen by the food industry's increased desire for sustainable and better food options. Businesses can strengthen their competitive advantage and cultivate consumer loyalty by matching their offerings with these preferences.

ANALYSIS OF COMPETITORS

One of the core components of market analysis is competition analysis, which entails assessing the advantages, disadvantages, opportunities, and dangers that other market participants present.

This analysis goes beyond direct competitors to encompass any organization that could affect market share or sway customer decisions. Tools like SWOT analysis (Strengths, Weaknesses, Opportunities, and Threats) are frequently used to evaluate rivals in-depth. Businesses can improve their strategies and pinpoint areas for distinction by studying the market positioning, unique selling propositions, and strategies of their rivals. Companies may quickly adjust to shifting market conditions and maintain an advantage in the competitive landscape by continuously watching their competitors.

FINDING SPECIALIZED MARKETS

Finding niche markets entails locating particular subsets of a larger market with unique requirements or preferences. With this tactic, companies can create a distinctive value proposition and cater to a niche market. A narrower client base, less rivalry, and the possibility of larger profit margins are characteristics of niche markets.

For example, in the fitness sector, tailored exercise regimens for specific populations, such as the elderly or expectant mothers, could represent a niche market. A customized approach to product creation and marketing, together with a thorough grasp of the target market, is necessary for successfully entering niche markets. Businesses may strategically carve out a distinctive character in the market and cultivate consumer loyalty by identifying and serving specialized markets.

CHAPTER THREE

ORGANIZING YOUR FARM TO GROW PEAS

SELECTING THE IDEAL SITE

Making the right geographical choice for your pea farm is essential to a good harvest. Peas grow best in soil that drains well and gets plenty of sunlight. Choose a location that gets at least six hours of sunlight per day. Photosynthesis, which is necessary for the growth and development of pods in pea plants, depends on adequate sunshine.

Furthermore, pick a spot that is shielded from strong winds because peas might be harmed by too much wind. Being close to a water supply is also helpful because regular watering is essential to the growth of peas.

Examine the land's terrain to guarantee appropriate drainage, since peas are susceptible to wet circumstances.

GETTING THE SOIL READY

A key component of pea growing, soil preparation has a direct impact on the general health and yield of your crop. Loamy soil that drains easily and has a pH range of 6.0 to 7.5—which is slightly acidic to neutral—is preferred by peas. Clear the chosen area of any debris, rocks, or weeds to start the soil preparation process. To increase the fertility and structure of the soil, add organic matter to it, such as compost or well-rotted manure. This improves moisture retention in addition to increasing nutrient content. To determine nutrient levels and make necessary adjustments, think about performing a soil test. Tilling the soil correctly helps to establish an environment that is conducive to the development of pea roots by promoting aeration.

HOW TO CHOOSE PEA VARIETIES

Selecting the appropriate pea types is essential to maximizing productivity and satisfying certain tastes. Snap peas, snow peas, and shelling peas are the three primary categories into which pea varieties can be generally divided. Snap peas are eaten with the pod as well as the immature peas; snow peas are harvested for their sensitive, flat pods; shelling peas are usually harvested when the seeds inside the pods reach maturity. When choosing pea types, take into account variables such as the intended purpose, local weather, and climate. Little Marvel, Sugar Snap, and Green Arrow are a few of the well-liked options. Observe growth patterns and disease resistance to make sure the types you choose support your farming objectives.

CROP ROTATION TECHNIQUES

To maximize pea yield, avoid disease development, and preserve soil fertility, proper crop rotation plans must be put into practice. Peas are a member of the legume family and are special because they work in harmony with bacteria that fix nitrogen in the soil to fix nitrogen in the soil. Use crop rotation to improve this nitrogen-fixing potential by planting peas in successive seasons along with non-legume crops.

To lower the danger of soil-borne infections, don't plant peas or other legumes in the same spot for at least two to three years. This method improves soil health generally and breaks the life cycle of pea-specific pests and illnesses. When there aren't any pea seasons, think about adding cover crops to the soil to help keep it structured and further enriched.

Cautious site selection, thorough soil preparation, deliberate crop rotation, and mindful pea variety selection are all necessary for successful pea farming. By keeping these fundamental ideas in mind, you may improve the general prosperity of your pea farm and cultivate peas in a favorable environment.

CHAPTER FOUR

INFRASTRUCTURE AND FARM EQUIPMENT

ESSENTIAL TOOLS FOR GROWING PEAS

Like any other agricultural enterprise, pea farming greatly depends on a few key pieces of equipment to ensure productivity and efficiency. A vital piece of machinery is the tractor, which is utilized for several jobs like planting, tilling, and plowing. Modern tractors with technology add to improved soil management in addition to time savings. Another essential instrument for pea farmers is a seed drill, which makes it possible to plant seeds uniformly and precisely while maximizing germination rates. Furthermore, harvesters made especially for pea crops expedite the harvesting procedure and increase yield collection efficiency.

SYSTEMS OF IRRIGATION

In agriculture, effective water management is critical, and irrigation systems are essential for pea growing. Specifically, drip irrigation systems provide a focused and water-efficient way to hydrate roots directly. This reduces the growth of weeds and stops soil erosion in addition to conserving water.

Moreover, sprinkler watering systems are frequently used, giving larger pea fields a wider coverage area. Improved yields and resource conservation are achieved through precision and ideal moisture levels for pea crops through the use of modern sensors and automation in irrigation equipment.

FACILITIES FOR STORAGE

Appropriate storage facilities are essential for maintaining pea crop quality and avoiding post-harvest losses following a successful harvest. Grain bins and silos are frequently used for bulk storage, shielding peas from pests and moisture in the environment.

When a market need emerges, these storage structures enable effective handling and distribution.

In addition, cold storage facilities are necessary to maintain the freshness of peas, especially in areas with warmer weather. Controlling the temperature and humidity in these storage areas aids in preserving the harvested peas' market quality and nutritional worth.

CONTROLLING PESTS

Pea crops are vulnerable to a range of pests that, if not controlled, can severely reduce production. To reduce the usage of pesticides, integrated pest management (IPM) techniques are frequently used. These tactics combine chemical, cultural, and biological control measures.

Predatory mites and ladybugs are examples of beneficial insects that are introduced to naturally control hazardous pests. Two cultural strategies that break the life cycle of pests and strengthen plant defenses include crop rotation and the use of resistant pea cultivars. Additionally, to reduce environmental effects and protect the ecosystem as a whole, pesticides should be used sparingly and by safety recommendations when needed. To ensure a healthy and productive crop, it is imperative to conduct routine monitoring of pea fields to rapidly identify and address any insect infestations.

CHAPTER FIVE

AGRICULTURAL METHODS

SOWING AND PROLIFERATION

The basic steps of cultivation, planting, and germination, are essential to the success of agricultural undertakings. The first step in the process is to choose premium seeds and make sure they are free of faults and illnesses. An appropriate seed selection is the first step toward a plant's healthy growth.

Given that they affect sunshine exposure and nutrient absorption, planting depth and spacing are important factors to take into account. Different techniques, including direct sowing or transplanting, are used by farmers based on the type of crop and the surrounding surroundings.

The critical stage during which the seed becomes a young plant is called germination. This process requires the right amount of soil moisture, temperature, and oxygen availability. To increase germination rates, farmers might apply methods such as pre-soaking seeds or using seed treatments.

It is essential to keep an eye on the surrounding conditions throughout this phase to encourage consistent and robust seedling emergence.

CROP UPKEEP AND CARE

For best growth, crop upkeep and care become critical as soon as seedlings appear. This includes controlling pests, fertilization, and watering. The kind of soil and the amount of water needed by the crop influence the irrigation method selection.

Water management is aided by precision agriculture technologies like automated systems and sensors. Fertilization is the process of giving plants the necessary nutrients, either naturally occurring or artificially produced, to ensure balanced nourishment for healthy growth.

One of the ongoing tasks in crop maintenance is pest management. Biological, chemical, and cultural controls are all included in integrated pest management (IPM) techniques, which reduce insect damage while maintaining ecological equilibrium. Another crucial component of crop upkeep is weed control, as it lessens competition for nutrients and sunlight. Plant health should be regularly monitored, and problems should be resolved quickly to ensure successful production.

METHODS OF HARVESTING

The final step in the cultivation cycle is harvesting, which requires precise timing. Different crops have different ideal times to harvest, which affects things like flavor, nutritional value, and market value. Harvesting can be done manually or mechanically, depending on the crop and production volume. Large-scale operations benefit from the efficiency of mechanical harvesters, although manual harvesting is frequently chosen for delicate crops or those that need to be picked carefully.

Harvesting methods also take into account post-harvest needs, like preventing crop deterioration and reducing losses. When crops are harvested and handled carefully, they are guaranteed to reach the market or processing facilities in the best possible shape, maintaining their worth and quality.

AFTER-HARVEST MANAGEMENT

The term "post-harvest handling" refers to a set of procedures used to preserve the grade and marketability of harvested crops. It entails packing, cleaning, and sorting, all of which improve the produce's appearance and marketability. To prolong shelf life and avoid spoiling, proper storage conditions are essential. These factors include controlling humidity and temperature.

Another important component of post-harvest management is transportation. Crops are delivered to their destination on time and in ideal condition thanks to effective logistics.

Perishable goods are frequently stored in cold rooms or transported in refrigerators; nonetheless, cautious handling is required to avoid cuts or other damage while in transit.

Post-harvest treatment progressively includes value addition, which includes procedures like washing, peeling, and packaging to satisfy customer preferences and market expectations. Sustainable methods, like better distribution and storage to cut down on food waste, are becoming more and more important in post-harvest handling plans. All things considered, careful attention to post-harvest treatment guarantees that the cultivation efforts provide premium, commercially viable products.

CHAPTER SIX

ECOLOGICAL FARMING METHODS

ORGANIC PEA FARMING

Committed to using natural and biological techniques to raise peas free of synthetic chemicals and genetically modified organisms (GMOs), organic pea farming is a sustainable agricultural strategy. To improve soil fertility, organic pea producers rely on organic inputs including compost, cover crops, and natural fertilizers. This approach places a higher priority on the well-being of the soil, crops, and other ecosystems while reducing its negative effects on the environment. Organic pea cultivation helps produce healthier and chemical-free peas for consumers by eschewing the use of synthetic pesticides and herbicides.

ECO-FRIENDLY PEST MANAGEMENT

Eco-friendly pest management, which focuses on reducing the use of toxic pesticides to control pests, is an essential component of sustainable farming techniques. A crucial tactic in environmentally friendly pest management is integrated pest management (IPM), which combines mechanical, cultural, and biological control techniques to preserve a healthy ecosystem.

Beneficial insects, crop rotation, and companion planting are methods used in organic farming to organically manage pest populations. By promoting biodiversity and lessening the negative effects of farming on the ecosystem, this strategy builds a more resilient and self-regulating agricultural system.

WATER CONSERVATION STRATEGIES

Sustainable farming methods place a strong emphasis on the economical use of water resources. Water conservation is a critical issue in agriculture. Water conservation techniques are used in a variety of ways, such as soil moisture monitoring, rainwater collection, and drip irrigation systems.

For example, drip irrigation optimizes water consumption efficiency by delivering water directly to the plant's root zone while reducing waste. Reducing reliance on outside water sources by collecting and storing rainwater for use in agriculture during dry spells is known as rainwater harvesting.

These water-saving techniques support farmers' adaptation to a changing climate while simultaneously promoting environmental sustainability.

Sustaining soil health is essential to sustainable farming methods because it promotes plant development and increases the resilience of ecosystems as a whole. Crop rotation, cover crops, and the use of organic amendments are examples of organic farming practices that serve to improve soil structure, increase nutrient content, and encourage beneficial microbial activity. Planting some crops during dormant seasons is known as cover cropping, and its goals include stopping soil erosion, controlling weed growth, and enriching the soil with organic content.

Crop rotation replenishes soil nutrients organically and breaks the cycle of pests and diseases. Sustainable farming increases long-term productivity and lowers the demand for synthetic inputs, resulting in a more resilient and balanced agricultural ecosystem by placing a high priority on soil health.

CHAPTER SEVEN

BUDGETING

MAKING A BUDGET FOR PEA FARMING

A key component of financial planning is creating a budget for pea farming, which gives a detailed picture of the costs and revenue that may be anticipated from growing peas. Farmers can manage resources more effectively and guarantee that all operational costs are covered when they have a well-structured budget. This includes figuring out how much seeds, fertilizer, pesticides, labor, equipment, and other running expenditures will cost. Pea producers can track their spending throughout the agricultural cycle, make well-informed decisions, and set realistic financial targets by developing a thorough budget.

ANALYZING COSTS

A key component of financial planning for pea farming is cost analysis, which entails a careful review of all costs related to cultivation. This covers indirect costs like overhead and administrative fees in addition to direct expenditures like inputs like fertilizer and seeds. Farmers can find areas where cost-cutting strategies can be used without sacrificing the quality of the yield by using cost analysis. Through long-term sustainability and profitability, this analytical technique helps to optimize the total financial performance of pea farming operations.

INCOME FORECASTS

Since they provide an estimate of the anticipated income from the sale of pea crops, revenue predictions are a crucial part of financial planning for pea farmers. These estimates are based on several variables, including past yield statistics, market conditions, and pea demand.

Farmers must take into account the fluctuations in market prices and project a realistic quantity of peas that they hope to sell. Precise revenue forecasts facilitate farmers in establishing suitable sales objectives, devising marketing plans, and matching their financial expectations with market conditions, all of which ultimately augment a more steady and robust financial standing.

HAZARD ASSESSMENT

Risk management is a vital component of financial planning for pea growing, as agriculture is inherently subject to many risks. Farmers face risks related to weather conditions, pests, diseases, market fluctuations, and other unforeseen events. Implementing risk management strategies involves identifying potential threats, assessing their impact, and developing plans to mitigate or cope with them. This may involve purchasing crop insurance, diversifying crops, or incorporating sustainable farming practices that reduce environmental risks.

A robust risk management plan enhances the resilience of pea farming operations, safeguarding against financial losses and ensuring a more stable financial future.

Financial planning for pea farming encompasses budgeting, cost analysis, revenue projections, and risk management. Through meticulous budgeting, farmers can allocate resources effectively, while cost analysis enables the identification of areas for optimization. Accurate revenue projections facilitate informed decision-making, and robust risk management strategies ensure resilience in the face of uncertainties. These interconnected concepts collectively contribute to the overall financial health and sustainability of pea farming operations.

CHAPTER EIGHT

TECHNIQUES FOR MARKETING AND BRANDING YOUR PEAS

Marketing requires branding, which is more than just coming up with a catchy tagline or logo. It entails giving your good, service, or in this example, peas, a unique identity. A distinctive value proposition is communicated and an emotional bond is made with the target audience through effective branding. When it comes to "Branding Your Peas," take into account components like the history of your peas, the product's quality and source, and the ideals your brand stands for. In a crowded market, a strong brand may help your company stand out by establishing trust and loyalty among customers.

MAKING A STRATEGY FOR MARKETING

The road map that directs your efforts to successfully market and sell your products is a thorough marketing plan. Your marketing objectives, target market, strategy, and techniques should all be described in this plan. To start, gather information about consumer preferences, market trends, and rivals by performing market research. Establish a clear Unique Selling Proposition (USP) and create messaging that appeals to the needs of your intended audience. Both online and offline channels should be included in your marketing strategy to provide a comprehensive approach to reaching a wide range of consumers. Review and tweak your plan frequently to keep up with shifting consumer trends and market conditions.

ONLINE AND OFFLINE MARKETING CHANNELS

To optimize reach and engagement in the connected world of today, a successful marketing plan makes use of both online and offline channels. Social media sites, email marketing, content marketing, and search engine optimization (SEO) are examples of online channels. These digital channels provide data-driven optimization, real-time engagement, and exact targeting. On the other hand, audiences that might not be as engaged with digital media can be reached through offline channels like events, traditional print media, and collaborations with physical retailers. Maintaining equilibrium between digital and traditional media platforms guarantees a thorough and efficient marketing strategy.

FORMING ALLIANCES

Forming alliances is a calculated step that can boost your pea brand's success. To broaden your consumer base and reach new markets, partner with distributors, merchants, or other businesses that complement each other's offerings.

Influencers and brand ambassadors who share your beliefs and can tell their audiences about your products are also possible partners.

When choosing partners, make sure that their goals and brand values are in line, creating connections that will benefit both parties. By utilizing partnerships, you can benefit from pooled resources, chances for cross-promotion, and elevated reputation as a result of affiliation with well-known organizations. Developing and maintaining relationships is a continuous effort that can greatly aid in the expansion and long-term viability of your pea brand.

CHAPTER NINE

LEGAL ASPECTS OF REGULATIONS FOR PEA FARMING

A wide range of regulations, varying depending on the jurisdiction, apply to the management and cultivation of pea farms. These rules are intended to safeguard the safety and quality of the peas that are produced and to encourage fair competition in the agricultural industry. Pea farmers are subject to regulations for soil conservation, pesticide use, and crop rotation. Furthermore, certain laws about pea labeling and marketing may exist to safeguard customers and preserve market integrity. To prevent fines or operational problems, farmers must be aware of these restrictions and adopt procedures that comply with the law.

LICENSES AND PERMITS

To engage in pea farming, people or organizations usually need to acquire the required licenses and permits from the appropriate authorities. These documents, which can include approvals about water rights, land usage, and crop-specific laws, function as formal authority to engage in farming activities. Providing thorough plans for farming activities, proving compliance with environmental regulations, and paying relevant taxes are all possible steps in the licensing process.

Getting the licenses that pea growers need is essential to operating lawfully and laying the groundwork for a compliant and sustainable agricultural enterprise.

RESPECT FOR ENVIRONMENTAL STANDARDS

Following established guidelines is crucial for sustainable and ethical farming methods, as pea cultivation, like any other agricultural activity, has an impact on the environment. Regulations about the environment may address topics like pesticide and fertilizer use, soil conservation, and water consumption.

It is anticipated that farmers will embrace environmentally friendly practices, like water-efficient irrigation systems, crop rotation, and environmentally friendly insect management strategies. Adherence to these guidelines guarantees the sustainability of the environment and also assists in reducing the likelihood of legal problems resulting from breaking environmental laws.

PROTECTION AGAINST PEA FARMS

Insurance is essential for reducing the hazards connected to pea farming. Crop diseases, market swings, and weather-related catastrophes are just a few of the variables that farmers must deal with. A financial safety net is provided by having the right insurance coverage in case of unanticipated events that could negatively impact the pea harvest.

Pea farm insurance may include protection against liability, crop loss, equipment damage, and business disruption.

To customize coverage that sufficiently safeguards their activities, farmers must carefully evaluate the risks that are unique to them and collaborate with insurance providers. Pea producers may strengthen their resilience and protect their livelihoods from unforeseen obstacles by putting comprehensive insurance in place. This will help to create a more stable and sustainable agricultural economy.

CHAPTER TEN

PROSPECTS FOR PEA FARMING'S FUTURE

EMERGING TECHNOLOGIES

Emerging technologies are revolutionizing traditional agricultural methods in the field of pea production. For example, precision agriculture maximizes crop management by utilizing drones, sophisticated sensors, and data analytics. This gives pea producers remarkable precision in monitoring plant conditions, irrigation levels, and soil health. Furthermore, pea varieties with improved resistance to pests and diseases are being developed with the assistance of genetic engineering and biotechnology, which will increase crop output and quality overall.

A more connected and effective agricultural environment is being fostered by the integration of Internet of Things devices with smart farming equipment, allowing for real-time monitoring and decision-making.

MARKET INNOVATIONS

There have been major market innovations in the pea-growing sector that are changing the dynamics of production, distribution, and consumption. Pea protein is in high demand as a flexible and sustainable substitute for animal proteins due to consumer preferences for plant-based proteins.

In response to the increased demand for plant-centric diets, innovative pea-based products have been developed, including pea protein isolates and pea-based meat alternatives. Furthermore, improvements in processing technology are making it easier to extract and use substances generated from peas, which increases the number of uses in the food and beverage sector.

A more robust and adaptable industrial landscape is being created by the cooperation of farmers, researchers, and food makers.

ADAPTING TO CLIMATE CHANGE

Adaptive measures are required to offset the impact of climate change, which presents a tremendous challenge to pea growing. Traditional growing seasons and pest dynamics are being impacted by temperature, precipitation patterns, and the frequency of extreme weather events fluctuating.

As a result, pea growers are implementing climate-smart techniques, such as using drought-resistant pea varieties and modifying planting dates to correspond with shifting weather patterns. To preserve water supplies, sustainable water management techniques including rainwater collection and drip irrigation are also being used.

Within the agricultural community, collaborative projects are promoting knowledge and best practice exchange, enabling a group effort to strengthen resilience against the challenges presented by climate change.

PROSPECTS AND DIFFICULTIES

For those involved in the industry, the changing pea-growing landscape offers both opportunity and problems. On the plus side, pea producers now have access to new markets thanks to the growing demand for plant-based protein sources. Growing consumer consciousness about how food choices affect the environment has led to a greater interest in plant-based, sustainable diets, which has elevated peas to the status of a precious commodity. However, many farmers face obstacles due to issues including erratic weather patterns, unpredictability in the market, and the requirement for significant investment in the adoption of new technologies. It is still very difficult to strike a balance between pea farming's economic sustainability and sustainable practices, which calls for a careful balance between immediate financial gain and long-term environmental protection.